SATAN at my WINDOW

A True Story

By Maureen Hughes
with Adrian Littlefield

Copyright, 2018 Maureen Hughes

All rights reserved. No part of this book may be reproduced or utilized in any form or by any means, electronic, or mechanical, including photocopying, recording or by any information storage or retieval system without written permission of author.

Cover design by Sara Woodard
Typesetting by Sara Woodard
Cover and text photographs courtesy of the author.
Printed by Kindle Direct Publishing

ISBN-13: 9781791943219
Library of Congress Control Number: Pending

Contact the author at:
maureenhughes@yahoo.com

This book is dedicated to Adrian Littlefield. What a joy and unforgettable experience for me to know you!

A Cherokee Prayer...

May the Warm Winds of Heaven blow softly on your home and the Rainbow always touch your shoulder.

Other books by Maureen Hughes

TRUE CRIME
THE COUNTESS AND THE MOB
SINS OF THE SOUTH
RIVER OF SHAME

HISTORIAL FICTION
TINY MOCASSINS
A FIRE STILL BURNS
THE INDIANS GENERAL
THE OTHER SIDE

acknowledgements

Though numerous medical and judicial journals have covered the quest for answers to why Charles Whitman committed the atrocity he did, articles that speculated on the 'why's', news coverage that presented all known facts of the victims, books and two movies nothing has been put in print about the life of the second victim, Adrian Littlefield. His life before and after the incident and most of all his miraculous healing despite Satan's venomous, unswerving attempts to beat God's plan for him. It is my wish that *SATAN AT MY WINDOW* be a catalyst to use by those who have suffered tremendous occurrences in their lives that have left them with no hope, no will to go on with their lives, with no closure.

The journey to write this book, unlike any other I've written, has enhanced my relationship with God and opened my eyes to the realization that Satan is everywhere.

The author is most grateful for the assistance of Pastor Louis Green of Defiance, MO in helping Adrian to relive the time so the events could be presented in this book. Pastor Lowell Goins for the encouragement he gave to Adrian. Greg Littlefield, Scott Littlefield, and Brenda Littlefield Tice were especially generous with their time, thoughts and memories. It has added so much to the book. My sincere gratitude to each of you! As always I thank Sara Woodard whose patience with me is worth an award! And most of all a hug for Adrian who allowed the pain to return to tell the story of God's presence in his life and His healing hand that is still with him today.

preface

In the fall of 2017, I received a call from Pastor Lowell Gowins of Rosiclare, Illinois. I had met Pastor Gowins at one of my previous book signings. He asked if I would consider writing a book on a dear friend of his...Adrian Littlefield. Adrian was one of the survivors of the 1966 University of Texas clock tower shootings. Recalling the incident vividly, I wondered what made this man stand out for a book. There had been at least one book written, a movie and television documentary covering the subject. Pastor Gowins stated Adrian had an amazing story that hadn't been written about and everyone should hear. It wasn't *just* about recovering from the massive injuries.

Leaving the fertile farmland of central Illinois, I traveled Route 94 through the beautiful Missouri countryside of lush rolling hills peppered with acres of vineyards to Defiance, Missouri for an arranged meeting with a man I had never met.

A seemingly gentle man, small in stature, twinkling eyes and a broad smile greeted me before his outstretched hand shook mine. Unbeknownst to me this was the beginning of hearing the story of the heinous crime against, the miraculous healing, and an unexpected visitor of Adrian Littlefield. Like the state, the University of Texas, in Austin, Texas, has and is a global impact over 131 years. "What starts here...changes the world." The university's motto has stood the challenges over the decades. Through the glow of national and worldly accomplishments, the shadow of tragedy stained the university.

There are no layers of allegory in what happened that August day in 1966. Few in the nation were left untouched by the carnage former Marine Charles Whitman left behind at the base of the University's 307-foot-tall clock tower. The country was still numb from the killing of a loved President. No other event, of this caliber, had happened in the United States to date. That day one man changed the enhanced, peaceful landscape of the university to one of horror, leaving the massacre an enduring part of Austin, Texas' history.

On that sweltering August day 16 people were in the process of shaping their lives with their first job. Others their first year as college students, a couple who just days earlier, recited their vows to share their lives together, were enjoying life, and one who was hoping to carry the next generation full term. Most of the victims were strangers to each other... *all* were strangers to Charles Whitman. No rhyme or reason to any of the killings. All were like pawns on a chess board. Whitman's denouement of the lives of 16 people and the life-changing, permanent effects of 31 others has been chronicled in numerous passages. Traumatic events do not last for the minutes, hours or days they occur, but leave enduring scars on the mind and cause a person to constantly scrutinize everyone they meet and every situation they encounter. Those in Austin, Texas, that day in 1966 have sustained permanent social damage whether they were actual victims of the shooting, a friend or relative of a victim or the city at large.

Satan at My Window covers the life of the second person shot by Charles Whitman, his life-threatening injuries, his will to live through his trials with his exemplary diligence to survive and accept God's plan for him...*and* through the shadow of Satan's constant sardonic threats. Through Charles Whitman's warped thinking, he was providing an end to his belief that the world wasn't fit to live in. He instead left a community in shock, families torn apart and the Texas state flag flying at half-staff. During the next few weeks the city received an outpouring of sympathy and concern for the people who suffered the event.

But the story doesn't end with Whitman's sanguinary act.

Adrian's story goes way beyond the injuries he sustained from the shooting. Instead of a story of instant victorious testimonial about recovery and forgiveness, Adrian Littlefield suffered in his own hell for months. Besides the healing hand of God hovering over Adrian, the swirling fog of the devil kept pushing his way to the forefront of Adrian's recovery.

I dug into the memories Adrian has tried to keep buried. I've watched his expressions change from contentment over having the story written to the appearance of pain in his eyes and the tightening of his jaw when he tells his story. He suddenly looked tired and worn in remembrance of those 90 minutes he lived in the depths of hell.

With Adrian's friends, Pastor Lowell Gowins and Louis Green, urging me to write his story, it is Adrian's hope that others who have lived through horrific events, suffered tremendous occurrences in their lives that have left them with no hope, no will to live and no closure, and the loved ones that stood by them, find the solace he did in the Lord. For those who have witness tragedy in the schools, churches and public places reach out to friends and God for reassurance and comfort in the healing process. This, too, is my prayer.

In 1881 retired Civil War Illinois Cavalry Captain Isaac Conroe, left Houston, Texas in search of land to pursue his lumber business. Stopping in Montgomery County, he purchased a tree- covered tract of land. Within a few short years, he had a profitable business outside of a community which would eventually bear his name. With the increased demand for lumber the town of Conroe, Texas grew. Homes were built, a school and post office followed. In December 1904 the community was officially incorporated. At the height of his career, Isaac Conroe employed 700 people, and his lumber and sawmill business was listed as the 1st in modernized lumber manufacturing plant and the 2nd most significant company in the south.

3

But the wealth of Conroe was attributed to George W. Stroke who discovered oil in 1931. An oil operator from St. Louis, Stroke, too financially strapped to develop the oil, contracted Exxon, Texaco and smaller companies to complete the project. Hints of a progressive community appeared. Soon a hotel, courthouse, newspaper, and drug store graced the main streets. With the oil boom and hundreds of oil men and speculators taking residence the population grew to 2,000 putting Conroe, Texas on the map.

A stubborn community with no desire to fail, the town of Conroe survived two fires that destroyed the business district both times, two world wars, lumber mills failing and oil veins drying up couldn't turn it into a ghost town. In the early 1960's Conroe had a population of 10,000. It boasted having more millionaires per capita than any other town in the United States.

About 13 miles outside of Conroe, LC Littlefield and Bonnie Ruth Beeson Littlefield made a home for their family of three sons. At a very young age Adrian's grandmother, Azilee Wells Littlefield, had changed his father's name from Leonard Charles to just LC mostly from bitterness over her divorce from Adrian's grandfather. Therefore, his Dad was forever referred to as just LC Littlefield. And so, Adrian's story begins.

one

"A man who has friends must himself be friendly, but there is a friend who sticks closer than a brother." Proverbs 18:24

My childhood was happy. I and my two brothers came from a solid, loving, Christian family. One of Dad's recurring utterances was, "God's purpose will prevail in all of us. Some of us will adhere to it...others will ignore it." The memory of these words would come back to me in periods of desperation that I would experience throughout my life.

My heritage, at least a part of it, is Cherokee. I don't know how far back or much about it other than what I have been told by my paternal grandparents. But I do know that George Littlefield, a Confederate Army officer and wealthy cattleman, was a major contributor to the Austin campus of the University of Texas and funded the Littlefield Fountain that rest on the quad grounds by the Administration building. The fountain was dedicated to the memory of former students who died in World War 1 and to honor long lost kinfolk. The fountain flows day and night and is a memorable sight at night when lights turn the water to shimmering gems and accent the fountain. Our home was small and simple...5 rooms that were built from the ground up with native trees by my maternal grandfather and my father. There was always laughter in the home and more so when many of the relatives that made up the large Littlefield family were there. My father, an only child, was reared by a moonshiner who was known to be mean and disrespectful. Grandfather Littlefield named my father Leonard Charles Littlefield at birth, but Dad's mother had his name changed to LC *just* LC at an early age. The two of them ended their marriage in a bitter divorce. My mother, Bonnie, on the other hand, had three brothers and six sisters so family gatherings were quite an occasion!

Dad worked in the oil fields around Conroe when I was very small. Later, being a self-taught welder, he acquired a respected reputation in the field along with working with concrete. Mom, a beautiful woman, both inside and out, was the heart and warmth of our family. She was a proven seamstress and created most of the clothing for myself and my brothers from cotton feed sacks though you wouldn't have known the material's humble beginning. She always prepared nutritious meals for the family. My maternal grandfather raised a variety of vegetables that grew on some of the small acreage he owned. The produce was sold to neighbors in the area and to some businesses in town. Thus, we were never without good, fresh food.

Our life was simple and entertainment much the same. As a family we enjoyed listening to the radio and I and my brothers specifically liked the Houston Colt 45's. We didn't own a TV. We weren't a wealthy family in the sense that we had money, but we had a closeness throughout and wanted for nothing.

A small community church of no distinct denomination rested deep in the wooded area around us. A good 4-5 miles away, we and most of the Littlefield family attended it. A Christian life was engrained in myself and my brothers early in life. I attribute this to not only our parents but our pastor Jimmy Tomplait. I should note here that the church remains to this day though larger with almost 500 members. But back then, in that church, is where I received my early devotion to God.

Attending church and our involvement in related functions was looked forward to by all of us. Both of my grandfathers were alcoholics and Grandfather Beeson also suffered from tuberculosis. He regularly attended church despite his health issues. At one service he gave his heart to God and was healed that very night...never to suffer again from alcoholism or tuberculosis.

Dad usually didn't sit with the family during a church service but stayed outside, leaning against a pine tree, to make sure I and my brothers behaved. All he had to do was snap his fingers, should we become mischievous, and we straightened up!

Christmas was always special to our family. Each year the children that attended the church put a seasonal skit on that was the entertainment. This was followed by everyone receiving a brown paper sack filled with an apple, orange and hard candy... something we, as kids, really looked forward to. It was a good and memorable time. Christmas at home was just as exciting. Mom and Dad, though frugal, gave each of us one gift that we *really* wanted. For me it was a 24-inch Western Flyer bicycle. I didn't have to be told to try it out! Naturally, I wanted my friends to see it and our home was one where friends liked to congregate. My mother always welcomed my friends and they liked her as well. They didn't mind me leaving the games we were playing to go and help her should she need assistance with something. Either my friends waited on me or came to help too if they could.

After working in the oil fields all day, Dad would come home and care for the chickens and cows. My brothers and I managed to engage him in playing ball with us before he did his evening chores. He *always* had time for us. Changing clothes after chores, he took his place at the head of the table. I helped Mom put the meal on the table and washing the dishes, if needed afterwards. Both parents taught us good table manners that were practiced at every meal. At the same time, respect for my mother and her life of raising us was easy to do through the example Daddy gave. There were disagreements between my parents on occasion, but Dad never yelled at any of us. It was a practice we all learned and have practiced in our own lives. My brothers and I learned early on the importance of *family* and the importance of keeping it *foremost* in our lives.

LC Littlefield boxed when he was a young man. He didn't do

it professionally but used it to teach self-discipline. Of course, this trait was passed on to me. Something that isn't always easy to follow.

My father enjoyed hunting and at the tender age of seven he asked me to go with him. I wanted to go. His purpose at my tender age was for me to earn his confidence and my respect for him. You see, a bond must form between a father and son… there has to be a friendship…a special *love* between them. On the first trip together Dad explained that there would be a lot of walking to find the game we were hunting. He stressed that I needed to be sure I wanted to go and because of so much walking he wasn't going to carry me! I was sure I could handle it but after what seemed miles of walking my legs grew tired. I sat on a fallen tree log and said, "Dad my legs are tired, I can't go any further." I began to cry. Dad said, "No… you have to walk, son. You must be man enough to finish everything you start." So I got up and walked further with him, but my legs began to hurt and once again I cried. Dad knelt down and said to me, "Son, I want to teach you a lesson today. There will be a person in your life…a very special person that will be there for you no matter what. A friend that will help you and never put you down. A friend that you can count on at any hour of the day or night." A few moments later he picked me up, put me on his shoulders and carried me back to the car. Yes, that was the kind of man my dad was…my friend. As I grew older I started trapping small animals for their pelts. In one season I had enough mink and raccoon pelts that after I sold them I had made $72.00. I thought I was rich!

I was around 7 years old, sitting in a church pew, listening to the message of the minister that spoke from the pulpit at the front of the church. He spoke of the end of time and stated what the Bible said it would be like. Everything he said touched my heart. Even if I thought of doing something wrong I felt the hand of God on me and wiped the thought from my mind. I remember the words the minister spoke when he said, "God's purpose will prevail in all of us...some of us will adhere to it and others will ignore it." I didn't know that my future included me destined to be a minister. To this day I feel a great compassion for people who have not been taught the love of God. I wanted to be the kind of minister that preached an inclusive gospel. One that reached *all* people...rich, poor, educated, illiterate. It was my will and desire, even at that tender age, to do whatever work is necessary to *please* God and leave me satisfied with *my* life.

Around 8 or 9, I showed all the symptoms of polio. Never medically diagnosed with the debilitating disease, the constant fatigue took over, the loss of appetite hit me and the weakened desire for anything. Mom prayed for me to be healed and asked our pastor to come to our home to pray along with me. God touched me, and I was healed! I ate like there was no tomorrow and when Dad was due home that evening I *ran* to the highway to meet him! Everyone was so excited at my recovery.

Dad held a firm hand on his sons but was never mean to any of us. I can vividly remember four times in my years at home that he whipped me, and I deserved every one of them! He wore a clear plastic belt and at age 17, after I disobeyed him and was very unkind to him over something serious that he had taught me not to do, he called me into the bedroom, removed his belt and whipped me. During the whipping Dad would say "I love you. I love you." He whipped me until the belt broke in four pieces! I didn't *believe* that and certainly didn't *love* him at the time. I thought that when I got big enough I would leave this house and never come back! I never committed any crimes or did anything *really* bad...but none the less deserved every one of those whippings! Neither my mother or father ever hesitated to tell us they loved us. And little did I know that just two years later I would need someone nearer to me than any other person I knew. This same man that had whipped me with his belt... that left welts on my legs...would be at my side during some of the darkest hours of my life.

I was never one to play hooky...until I reached high school that is! I especially liked being able to read books. The first six years of elementary school were cherished as I had very influential teachers. They influenced me by teaching more about life than I had experienced on my own. I loved reading and read every book I could get my hands on. Rudyard Kipling held my attention in his series on dogs. Finishing elementary school and high school in Conroe allowed access to the monthly book mobile that made its way through town. I grabbed all the books I was permitted to take for the month. It didn't take long for my teachers to see something in me and I'm sure it was due to my parental guidance through my formative years. I didn't smoke, drink or curse and that seemed to impress them.

Dad took night jobs through the years that kept him away from home two or three weeks at a time. I was the man of the house during those periods. I helped my mother when ever needed and felt important with my new position in the family. On one winter night, when the ground was frozen and cold temperatures sent a chill through the house, my mother woke me because of a strange noise at the front door. Having only my BB gun for a weapon we approached the door. The sound continued periodically. With my BB gun in shooting position Mom opened the door just enough to stick the barrel out. Much to our surprise my uncle's mule stood outside kicking at the door! Apparently, he got loose and came to our house. Reason unknown!

Continuing my schooling brought high school graduation which was welcomed as I could now start my dream of serving God as a minister. I was 17...searching for a new venue and experiencing a typical male's interest which was *girls*! At 18, like all young American men eighteen years old I needed to register for the draft. The Viet Nam war was still a reality and though I met the requirements for registration, my service to my country would *never* happen.

I wanted to exercise my new-found independence so, with

my parents understanding, I left home and rented a one-room apartment in Humble, Texas for $35.00 a week. I had a job at Armour Packing company and loved my life! I only stayed at the apartment three nights as my landlady wouldn't stay away from the stairs and my apartment door! I quickly went home to my old room. The family was glad to have me home, but Dad made it clear the same rules applied as they did before I left. Understood!

Growing up was an adventure sometimes. I had it all... a family that I loved and loved me, part-time jobs that kept money in my pocket, a good education under my belt, excited about attending college and at age nineteen...I committed my life to God. I was driven by the desire to help people who were hurting. This meant those who lived as saints and those who lived as sinners. While attending Texas Bible College in Houston, Texas I applied to Pasadena Independent School District for a custodial position to help with college expenses. During the application process, Louis Green, a friend that I met during my studies at the Texas Bible College, was also applying. Sure enough...we both were hired and had the fancy title of Custodial Engineer. Pretty high class for the two of *us*! My paternal grandmother offered to pay for studies in a secular college... she had dreams of me becoming a doctor, you see. Mom, being a devout believer in God, believed I was like Moses...a proper child. In telling my grandmother being a doctor was not my goal...she withdrew her offer to finance my college education.

I attended classes but soon realized that was not where I belonged as there wasn't any bible instruction. After some time, I felt a compelling call to leave seminary and become an Evangelist. Something else caught my eye during a revival service at a church in Austin, Texas. There she was, a beautiful girl sitting in one of the pews. I introduced myself and she told me her name was Brenda Wilkerson. We talked awhile. She had graduated from high school weeks earlier and was working in the clerical department at the University of Texas in Austin. I got up the nerve to ask her out which she accepted. We began seeing a lot of each other and both of us fell in love. Late July 1966 we were married in my home church in New Caney. It was a small wedding as I had another revival service to hold in a nearby town yet that night. We talked of my desire to do evangelism work as I felt it was another calling from God. Brenda understood and supported my decision. Everything was going like clockwork...married life seemed to suit both of us!

We celebrated our 9TH day of marriage by rising early the morning of August 1, 1966. Dad drove us the 200 miles to the Austin campus. Brenda had a paycheck waiting for her in the clerical department. We needed to pick up her car which had been a graduation gift from her parents. We had left her car at her parents' house when we had the wedding. Dad was going to re-finance her car in his name as Brenda's parents were not happy with the marriage. Once the business at the bank was over Dad would pick us up, we would have lunch and go home.

Coming out of the Tower, Brenda and I were holding hands. We had walked about fifty steps when I started teasing her about something and laughing about it. Then, laughing, I gently poked her in her left side. She moved slightly to her right. At the same time a sharp, *shattering* explosion was heard!

two

> "...the whole world lies under the sway of the evil one." 1 John 5:19

In the town of Lake Worth, Florida, Margaret Whitman and Charles Whitman Jr. left the hospital with their first-born son, Charles Joseph Whitman. He was the oldest of three sons. The Whitman home was rarely a happy one as Mr. Whitman was known for his violent temper and domestic violence toward his wife, Margaret, and later his sons.

Charles' father had been abandoned by his father at age 6. His mother, unable to provide financial support placed him and his two brothers in the Bethesda home for boys in Savanna, Georgia. His father lived there for nine years and was used to strict physical discipline. As a man he used the same tactics with his wife and sons for no other reason than to cover his own inadequacies and failures. He bragged publicly about being a self-made man. Though he provided well for his family, mistakes and failures *in* them or *by* them were unacceptable and corrected by punishments of various kinds.

Mr. Whitman worked as a plumbing contractor in the Lake Worth, Florida area and his mother was a homemaker who saw that her three sons were involved in the usual childhood activities. All the boys were taught proper manners and shared the religious training their mother had grown up in. As Roman Catholics, Charles and his two brothers were altar boys at Sacred Heart Roman Catholic Church. He served as pitcher for his school's ball team and manager of the football team. Besides the after-school activities Charles had a lucrative paper route. Neighborhood mothers would comment that they could only hope their sons would be like Charles Whitman.

Mr. Whitman took an interest in his sons' inquisitiveness in firearms. As an avid firearms collector, he taught them how to shoot and clean weapons at an early age. Outside of the hunting trips he took his sons on, this was the only quality time he spent with them. Because of his father's stern requirements to accept nothing but perfection, Charles became an avid hunter and skillful shooter.

During his elementary school years, he learned to play the piano and was considered an accomplished pianist. His outstanding achievement occurred when at age eleven he was accepted into the Boy Scouts. Whitman's juvenile activities were highlighted by becoming the youngest Eagle Scout, at the time, in 1942. For his personal spending Charles expanded his newspaper route. Saving his paper route money afforded him the purchase of a motorcycle to deliver the papers.

His studies at St. Ann's High School in West Palm Beach, Florida were above average, though his popularity with fellow students was mediocre. His teachers and students were knowledgeable about his intelligence, but it wasn't always shown in his grades. By his senior year his grades had improved, and he excelled above the other seventy-two seniors. At graduation in June 1959, he was seventh in his class. Celebrating with friends after graduation, Charles came home drunk and was severely beaten by his father. Unbeknown to his parents, Charles had enlisted in the United States Marine Corps weeks prior to graduation. The punishment he endured by his father cemented Charles' wish to leave the family. On July 6, 1959 he left home for an eighteen-month tour of duty at Guantanamo Bay.

During his time in the Marines, Charles received a Good Conduct Medal, Expeditionary Medal, and Sharpshooters Badge. He was accomplished in shooting moving targets and long-distance shooting. His goal was to apply for a scholarship with the United States Navy and Marines, so he could complete his college studies and become a commissioned officer. Achieving a high score on the examination, he was approved for schooling in Maryland. Completing the courses, he was granted approval to transfer to the University of Texas at Austin, Texas to major in mechanical engineering.

In 1961, Whitman began his course curriculum at the University of Texas. He didn't excel in the program as he had in his previous schooling. Besides his poor study habits, he was arrested with two friends for killing a deer without a permit and discovered butchering it in his dorm room shower. Because he was only fined for the offense he could remain at the university.

While a sophomore he met Kathleen Leissner. An education major at the university, the two dated when time allowed. The relationship blossomed and after five months, on July 19, 1962, twenty-year old Charles Whitman and Kathleen announced their engagement to their parents. On August 17, less than a month later, they married at her hometown church in Needville, Texas. Parents of both bride and groom attended the service and seemed happy with the marriage of their children.

Charles' performance in college after his marriage was insufficient and the scholarship was canceled. He was notified to report to Camp Lejeune, North Carolina for the remainder of his five-year enlistment. After reporting to Camp Lejeune, Whitman was promoted to Lance Corporal. Down deep he resented being expelled from college and began to gamble… not willing to hide it from his superiors. He was charged with a gambling offense, having possession of a personal firearm on base and making a threat to another Marine over a personal loan. He was court-martialed, demoted to private and sentenced to 30 days of hard labor. The demotion infuriated Whitman, causing him to assess the Marine Corps as time-wasting, unproductive, and disorganized. His wife Kathy tried to support his decisions though she was upset at his conduct.

Charles spoke highly of his wife to friends and in his personal diary that he regularly wrote in. For some reason he spoke of his opinions and thoughts of her more often since his court-martial. Whether this was how he *really* felt is not known. To support her he worked as a bill collector for the Standard Finance Company and later as a bank teller in Austin. Kathy kept her position as biology teacher at Lanier High School. To supplement their income after the school term she worked as a telephone operator until the school session began again in the fall.

During the month of March 1964, Whitman received a government-issued notice that his discharge date had been reduced by one year. The new date would be December 6,1964. The notice stated that he would be honorably discharged instead of the general discharge. According to the government the discharge was issued for the "convenience of the government." Charles' father would claim *he* was responsible for convincing the government to make the change.

During the 1964 Spring Semester enrollment period Charles changed his major from mechanical engineering to architectural engineering. For the next two years he took on extra jobs to support himself and Kathleen but didn't stay with any of them very long. He felt that he *really* needed to be a real estate agent. His thinking was he could make more money faster. This was just another one of Whitman's schemes. The job turned sour and he never received wages or commissions for any sales.

Charles began attending the First Methodist Church of Austin that Kathleen was a member of. He had not been a practicing Catholic, like he was raised, for several months. He found fault with many of the beliefs and felt hell was actually a person's time on earth.

The month of May 1966 brought more frustration to Charles. His mother decided to divorce his father. In the past she had talked of doing so but after another round of abuse she left him. Fearing being alone with her husband when she packed clothes for herself and young son, John, she asked Charles to come home to be with her when she was prepared to leave. Charles obliged and had a police officer park outside the home in case his father attacked Margaret. Months later Charles would comment that he hated his father and regretted his mother had stayed with him for 22 years of her life. Mr. Whitman eventually admitted to beating Margaret on a regular basis.

Margaret Whitman moved into apartment #505 at Penthouse Apartments, 1212 Guadalupe Street in Austin. The apartment was close to Charles and Kathleen and her hope was to start a new life. John, 17, had already left home due to the repressive hold his father had over him. Once Margaret was settled John moved in with her. Shortly after the move, John was arrested for throwing a rock through a store front window. At his court hearing the judge gave him the choice of paying a $25.00 fine or returning home to live with his father. John chose to pay the fine. Margaret found steady employment as a cashier at Wyatt's Cafeteria in Austin. During her employment there, C.A. Whitman sent her and Charles money to help support them.

The divorce between his parents added to Charles' mental frustration. Charles was aware of the cause of his mental state but didn't know how to overcome the frustration and separate it from his attitude toward his wife. To ease his frustration he would take his feelings out by beating Kathleen...more than once. Up to the last beating she had tried to help Charles in any way she could but soon realized he needed professional help.

Eventually, Charles agreed and made an appointment March 29, 1966, with Dr. Jan Cochrum at the University of Texas Health Center. After hearing Charles' story, he prescribed Valium and referred him to a staff psychiatrist, Dr. Maurice D. Heatly. Before his appointment with Dr. Heatly, Charles made efforts to control his temper and outbursts. During the first hour-long session, Charles told Dr. Heatly everything that troubled him and the on-going fear that he was becoming like his father. He hoped he could be cured. Dr. Heatly would later state that Charles was full of hostility. The doctor *did* write in his report that Charles spoke of going up into the tower with a deer rifle and shooting people. Dr. Heatly also stated that most psychiatrists will say patients have shared similar thoughts and feelings with them. For most it is just talk…and hard for a doctor to determine if it is just talk or an act that will be carried out. He made an appointment for Charles in one week and firmly told Charles to contact him anytime before the appointment if he wanted too. Charles did not return.

Several days before his appointment with the doctors, Charles and his brother John climbed the steps of the tower to survey the sights around them. At the time, they spoke of the vivid colors, the hues of green in the farm land, and the clean, sun-drenched buildings that made up the 232-acre Austin campus.

Sunday, July 31, 1966, Charles Whitman purchased several boxes of rifle ammunition, a pair of binoculars, and a knife. Once home he added his new purchases to the foot locker he had kept from his military days. Already placed in the locker was an arsenal of weapons and other items for personal use. Feeling satisfied that he had everything he needed he lowered the lid to the foot locker and secured it. Later in the afternoon he spent time with Kathleen, friends, and his mother saying nothing about his day to them.

Keeping a journal, Charles made entries describing physical changes that involved violent impulses and horrible headaches. His writing indicated that he had already planned further killings though not giving places nor days that this would happen. He wrote of killing Kathleen, his wife of four years. He wrote that he would kill her when he picked her up from her evening job. Whitman's reasoning was that he didn't want her to face the embarrassment his killing would cause. On the evening of the last day in July, Charles closed his journal when friends dropped by.

After a short visit with them he drove his 1966 Chevy to Kathy's summer work place. When her evening shift ended as a telephone information operator, she joined him, and they drove home. Whitman suggested they go to his mother's apartment. The night was hot, and Margaret had air conditioning. Kathleen decided to go home. She was tired and wanted to retire for the night. Letting her out of the car he drove to Austin's Penthouse Apartments. Inside his mother's apartment a struggle broke out between them. Overpowering Margaret, he stabbed her in the heart. Picking her lifeless body up, he placed her on the bed and covered her with sheets. Going to a desk, he took a piece of paper and wrote, "I have just taken my mother's life. I am very upset over having done it. However, I feel that if there is a heaven she is definitely there now...I am truly sorry...let there be no doubt in your mind that I loved this woman with all my heart." Whitman also left a note in first person on the apartment's front door for the apartment's caretaker. The note stated she was up late the night before and needed rest and that she didn't want to be disturbed. It was shortly after midnight, Monday, August 1.

Once inside their home, Kathleen removed her watch, wedding rings and dinner ring laying them on the dresser. She then removed her clothes and laid naked on the bed. This was her normal ritual for bed. The only lights were the lightning bugs outside their screened bedroom window and only a hint of a breeze.

Leaving his mother's apartment Charles returned home at 906 Jewell Street. Inside their bedroom, Charles saw his sleeping wife, took out his knife, bent over her, and stabbed her three times in the heart. He covered her with bed sheets. By 3:00 am, Charles had killed both his mother and wife.

When the Charles Davis hardware store opened at 9:00am the next morning Whitman went directly to the sporting goods department. He had a list of what he wanted to purchase. The list included 1-.30 caliber carbine with extra clips and numerous boxes of ammunition to fit other forms of firearms. He willingly told the sales staff that he was intending to travel to Florida to shoot wild hogs. He was prepared for the expense and not wanting to leave a paper trail, paid for his purchases in cash.

Earlier, at 7:15 am, Charles rented a mover's dolly. He had previously armed himself with other weaponry to the point of having an arsenal secured in his military foot locker. His final stop was to purchase Spam at a convenience store. At 11:00, just minutes before thousands of students would be changing class, he entered campus property and drove to the parking lot designated for campus officials and parked. Dressed as a maintenance crew employee he removed the dolly from the back seat and placed the foot locker on it. He pushed the dolly carrying the foot locker toward the elevator of the Clock Tower. As he approached the elevator two professors and two children emerged from the elevator. Whitman entered the elevator backwards pulling the loaded dolly in with him. He pressed the button that took him to the 27TH floor. He exited and pulled the loaded dolly up three flights of stairs to the 30TH floor. Whitman opened the door leading to the observation deck and was met by Edna Townsley, one of the Tower's receptionists. It is unclear what prompted the confrontation between them, but Whitman beat her, crushing her skull. He dragged her lifeless body across the room and hid her behind a couch. To prevent further people entering the area he secured the stairway with furniture. Charles Whitman would encounter six more people before he made it to the observation deck. Two he would kill. Once situated on the Tower deck he assembled his weaponry. Taking a position under the VI of the clock's south side, Charles could see hundreds of students walking to or from their classes. He studied the area then picked up the 30-6 rifle loaded it with 6mm shells and took aim. In the gun sights he saw a young couple laughing and holding hands just steps from the administration building below him. He took aim. At 11:48 a horrific explosion ricocheted through the quad. In a few seconds the young couple who had been laughing and holding hands were on the ground…shot!

SATAN AT MY WINDOW

three

Be alert and of sober mind. Your enemy, the devil, prowls around like a lion looking for someone to devour.
1 Peter 5:8

The impact of the first shot threw Brenda a few feet from me and grazed her left side. She froze in place and I could see she was injured. The gash on her left side was between eight and ten inches long. Blood was soaking through her clothing. Familiar with the sound of gun fire, I ran to her. As I moved in front of her, ready to push her down, a second shot rang out hitting me in the waistline area of my back blowing my insides out of me. As I was falling, I realized the shots were coming from the Clock Tower. I reached out and pushed Brenda to the ground. As I lay there trying to get my bearings I saw Claire Wilson shot. My eyes followed her as she went down. I knew we were behind a short wall leading to some steps. Claire was laying in the open and I couldn't get to her. The pain was excruciating in my entire body and I heard more gun fire hitting close to us from either side of the wall we were shielded by. Then I realized my left side wouldn't move. My left arm and leg would not move as my brain commanded them to do. My left side was paralyzed! The sound of the shots continued to fill my ears, alternating with the screams of horror from people around me. I laid still and could see people falling from being shot. I watched as some moved in agony...and others laid perfectly still.

Then I looked back at Brenda. This beautiful girl laying on the hot cement...her blood oozing out of her leaving a bright red trail in the midday sun. My pain was so intense my instincts were to close my eyes but Brenda, seeing how bad I was, continually talked to me to keep me awake. The temperature was 101 degrees that day and it felt like my insides that laid bare were frying on the hot concrete. I wanted to scream as the pain began to encompass my entire body. I wanted to *scream* with all my might as my body was burning, and I couldn't scream!

After what seemed hours, a young man who had just returned from Vietnam, I learned later, bent over me and asked if there was anyone he could contact. I told him Dad was waiting for us near the Littlefield Fountain. When the man found Dad, he told him to brace himself...that I had been shot in the back and wouldn't make it. He had seen too many soldiers shot where I was shot, and the ending wasn't good. I must tell you that, how sad I am that I never saw or heard from the soldier again.

Dad ran in a hail of bullets to cover the several yards behind Brenda and me. Whitman could see the three of us but that didn't stop Dad. My Dad...my *friend*, the man who had confidence in me...who *loved* me...ran... never thinking of the danger *he* was in but continued to run because one of his children was badly hurt and comforted us as best he could. Charles Whitman saw the movement and began firing in our direction as Dad tried to shield us from the gun fire and the boiling hot sun. He ran to Brenda first, a woman he hardly knew, and cradled her in his arms as her blood ran down where mine was pooling on the concrete. Then he leaned over where I was...rolled me over and gasped. Seeing how bad I was, looked away and wept. Sometime later when I recalled what Dad did I thought of John 15:13. Greater love hath no man than this; that a man lay down his life for his friend.

For an hour or so Dad kept vigil over the two of us. When he thought it was safe, Dad picked up my wife, bent low and hurried to an open window of a building. He lifted her through the window that was out of sight and range of Whitman. Laying there and watching I thought of what he had said two years earlier when he was whipping me and saying, "I love you". He did this not because he *knew* her but because he loved me, and *she* was my wife. He told me he would be back for me. I could see blood was still running on the cement and remembered I had a new shirt and boots on. A funny time to think of that!

Soon two men, innocent bystanders, came with a stretcher and Dad helped to place me on it. The stretcher had certainly seen better days. It had a split down the middle! All of us hurried behind a small building that shaded us from the scorching sun. I turned to him and said, "Daddy, I'm dying!" He said, "You have to live son...you *can not die!* You have to think of your wife, son. You have to think of your mother, but most of all you have to think of your *God and your call to the ministry!*" Soon an armored car backed up behind the building that shielded us. You see no ambulance could get through the barrage of bullets the sniper was firing. Dad was behind the stretcher ignoring the bullets fired at them because the mutilated body of his 19-year-old son was slipping away and because he *loved* me. Dad said to the stretcher bearers, "You get my son to safety and if you don't I will hold you responsible!"

The two men ran in a state of panic as bullets stirred the dust all around them. The two bystanders placed me in the armored car on the hot metal floor. I thought my body was frying. My feet hung outside not allowing the doors to close... all the time Whitman kept firing at it. Dad went with us as the armored car sped through the campus to the hospital. In the armored car Dad said to me, "If you do nothing else for me you live! You live for your wife, your mother and for your God!" The driver turned to look at Dad and said, "Mister whatever you do don't let your boy go to sleep." One of the men began to rub my arms and hands but the driver said you must do more. I remember the worn, calloused hand that slapped my face again and again to keep me conscious. He kept slapping and slapping until my face was red, and my eyes were blackened. He did this because he loved me and was willing to cause more pain to keep me alive. When I knew Brenda was being cared for I looked at my father and said, "Daddy, I know I'm dying...I can't take any more." Dad said, "Baby you can't die! Satan tries to take us...but sometimes death is not an option. You can't die! You have your ministry to fulfill!" But I knew Satan was present and continued to destroy me.

four

"For He will give his angels charge concerning you, to guard you in all your ways." Psalm 91:11

While on a routine traffic stop 23-year-old Austin police officer Billy Speed was summoned to the scene due to his close location to the shooting. Racing to the scene in his squad car and siren blaring he took a position where he joined Officer Jerry Culp. The two positioned themselves between two balusters. Whitman saw them through his rifle sights and fired hitting Officer Speed in the head almost decapitating him. He was taken to Brackenridge hospital where he was pronounced dead on arrival.

Ramiro Martinez, a 29-year-old Austin Police sergeant, stood in the kitchen of his home not far from the Austin University making a sandwich for lunch. He had less than three hours before his 3-11 shift started. A news alert on the TV caused him to glance at the TV screen: *At 11:48 this morning, a lone gunman began firing at anyone and everyone from the top of the University of Texas Tower. As of yet, the gunman has not been stopped or identified.*

Officer Martinez immediately called the department to see if he should report in early. His lieutenant ordered him to come in and assist in keeping traffic away from the university. When he arrived on campus it was obvious that traffic was already being diverted away. He parked his car and worked his way to the Jefferson Davis statue on the South Mall. From there Martinez could see several victims laying on the concrete. Realizing he was in the path of the shooter he cautiously eased his way to the tower to see if he had a shot at the gunman. When it was safe to do so he worked his way inside the tower and went straight to the elevator.

Getting off the elevator, within the tower on the 26TH floor, he climbed the steps that led to the observation deck. Behind him were Officer Houston McCoy and a civilian, Allen Crum, carrying a rifle. Sergeant Martinez forced the dolly that Whitman had used to block the Observation Deck away from the door and eased his way to a side where he could see Whitman. Officer McCoy fired at the west wall causing Whitman to turn and face the vicinity of McCoy and Martinez. McCoy fired again hitting Whitman. Whitman did not fall...Sergeant Martinez raised his drawn gun and fired one shot hitting Whitman. At 1:24 the shooting stopped, Whitman went down and did not get up. Forty-three people were shot, seventeen died including a little boy on his bicycle 4 blocks away and an unborn baby.

five

> *Paul, the apostle, said that there will be circumstances in your life that will alter the rest of your life.*
>
> *God is our refuge and strength, a very present help in troubled times.*
>
> **Psalm 46:1**

The emergency room at Breckenridge was divided into three areas to accommodate the victims as they were brought in. One area was for those who died before reaching the hospital or about to die. The second area was for those who needed medical treatment, but their injuries were not life threatening. Third, the area for the most critical that needed immediate surgery...where I was placed. The cry for God's protection was on my lips as I lay helplessly. Two doctors were evaluating victims in the third area. One of the two doctors thought I was never going to live and to move me to the area of already dead or dying. He wanted to move on to another victim but the other doctor, Dr. Nelson, felt something, and his mind would not let him close the book on me that fast. The first doctor argued saying no one could live with the wounds I had! Dr. Nelson, ignoring his comment ordered me to be taken to O.R. immediately! He later stated that he felt something special about me and wouldn't dismiss me.

In my first conscious moments in ICU, at Breckenridge Hospital, I couldn't see because my eyes were closed from the forceful attempts of my father to keep me awake during the trip to the hospital. For a short time I thought I was blind! How could I maneuver in the pulpit if I couldn't see? I had committed my life to God...all my life, my energy in God's cause for humanity. I removed the mask of pretense from my life when I said "yes" to His call. I couldn't see my mother and father. But as I lay on the edge of death I knew they were there and could hear the sweet voice of Mom singing the great hymn *Jesus Loves Me*. While she sang I felt the love only parents can give. When my eyes finally focused I could see Dad and Mom standing at my side. Dad leaned over me and talked to me. I felt something wet on my face and realized it was tears that came from him as he looked at my swollen cheeks and blackened eyes. He kept repeating how sorry he was, but he didn't want me to die.

As Dad talked to me I thought of the Bible story of Job. Job had everything a person could want. Wealth, a wonderful family and he was happy. Then Satan tells God that the only reason Job is faithful to him is because God has allowed him to prosper and has protected him. Satan suggests that God take everything away from Job believing Job would curse him. So Satan is allowed to test Job by taking his family, his wealth… everything of worth from Job…but Job remained faithful to God. God knew Job inside and out and knew nothing Satan could do would change Job's faithfulness no matter what. The biblical story proved that true Christians will persevere in their trials and tribulations if they remain faithful to God.

On the other side of the bed my mother moistened my cracked and bleeding lips. Fever had lasted a long time and *remained* high for a long time. As she did this the same sweet melody rose from her as she sang *Jesus Loves Me*. This was the most reassuring moment that later turned into our anthem of praise many times in the years that followed.

A doctor treating victims with injuries not of the depth as mine was brought in to treat Brenda. He assured her she would be fine. She was transported to Seton Hospital where other non-critical patients were taken. She was one of three taken there. I learned later that she had surgery and remained a patient for three days before being released with a good prognosis.

On August 2, I received a telegram from Preston

Smith, Lieutenant Governor of Texas, stating that all of Texas was grieving over the incident and that his thoughts and prayers were with me. He also stated that the facilities of his office were at my disposal and finally he hoped for a speedy recovery for me. I thought that was very nice.

Oh, I should mention that a few days after the shooting, my parents opened a letter from the draft board. I was to report to the induction center a few days later. Dad went in my place and tried to explain what had happened to me, but the board refused to accept the explanation. They threatened a warrant would be issued and possible arrest if I didn't appear. No doubt elaborate excuses were common place. Dad spoke with the surgeon who sent a letter stating my injuries and paralysis. That was the end of that issue.

For days I was in agony. No sleep for 3 nights. After 16 hours of surgery sleep would not come to me. Nothing in medical science was effective. Soft singing didn't work. The non-stop screaming of ambulances arriving at the hospital, the crying of family members in adjacent rooms over the loss of loved ones, the noises that could be heard throughout the floor I was on…I could *not sleep!* I needed solace of some kind. Across the room I saw a murky film pass by, go to my window and dissolve. At 3:30 am, on one of the few nights in over two months that my mother wasn't there, I turned to my mother-in-law and told her to call the preacher. I needed him to find God for me. She said, "Adrian, it's 3:30 in the morning…what preacher is going to come at this hour?" But he did! That man of God came…and he entered the room with faith in his heart. He didn't care that I was a Conroe, TX country boy. He didn't care that no one knew me. He placed his hand on my forehead and immediately said, "I love you. I have never in my life felt the presence of the devil like I have by touching you! Satan is trying to *kill* you! In the name of Jesus Christ I command *you, Satan,* to leave this room!" Before he could remove his hand, I was fast asleep.

A few days later I thought I should try to get out of bed. I couldn't! I couldn't even move enough to *try* to get out. I suddenly realized that I would never be able to pursue the call of God the rest of my life. After a stay of a few days in the ICU the word had gotten out that I was studying to be a minister. Families of other patients began to lean on me to pray for their loved ones. The ICU back in 1966 was a ward, not individual rooms but a long room with curtains separating each patient from other patients. Miss Karen Griffith, another victim who was shot in the lung, was 17 years old and a student in the high school that Kathleen Whitman taught at. She was in the adjacent cubicle and I could see her. She would plead with her big blue eyes for any help possible. During her time there I never once saw her eyes blink or close. She was in a desperate condition as were all the patients in that part of the facility! She died seven days later. Mary Gabour who was just a few beds from me lost her son by Whitman's bullets and she was left blind for life. I remember her praying to God to give her sight back.

The atheist mother of Claire Wilson, a severely wounded victim, would visit each time I was able to converse! She was shocked at her daughter's language and God-loathing attitude. Most days I could hear Claire yelling. She was at the opposite end of ICU. I tried to encourage her to understand that things would get better but her only response would always be vile cursing. Claire's mother would pass my cubicle almost every day and ask me to pray for "my Claire" as she would say. Claire found her mother's request odd as she was a professing atheist. Claire's future was going to be difficult. Her bitterness was understandable due to her condition. Her unborn baby died when Whitman shot her in the abdomen. Her boyfriend was completely decapitated by Whitman's gun. Watching her it seemed she would have rather died than face the coming days. I saw many of the prayers for others answered; thus I reconciled myself to the reality that I would, perhaps, fulfill my call in an awful physical condition. I don't think I ever considered quitting in my dream of preaching God's word.

Satan didn't appear every day, but I could hear his insane and horribly frightening laughter almost daily. The day I was to get out of bed and actually stand up, Satan sat on my window sill. Three or four men came into my cubicle to help me stand up. When I stood great amounts of fluids gushed from the lower openings on me. Mostly the fluids were pus and rotten smelling corruption. Once again, I realized my dire circumstances. At 19 I had never been in a hospital for any reason and now I sensed the fact that I would never leave...*alive*!

When the attendants placed me back in bed I could hardly keep it together. I cried uncontrollably. My father, who was with me during this raised my paralyzed leg in a more comfortable position with the paralyzed foot flat on the bed. Looking over at my window I saw the copy of David Wilkerson's book entitled *The Cross and the Switchblade* sitting on the sill. I was hoping to start reading it later when the charge nurse came in. Little did I know that would be the last time she attended to me! She looked at me and exclaimed, "How repulsive. Who ever heard of such a thing!" What bothered her was the book on the window sill! The nurse unleashed an ugly barrage of unrequested exasperation. She looked at me and proceeded to pound on the knee of my bent leg until it gave way and was flat on the bed. Pain racked my entire body! A short time later Dr. Nelson, who had been my physician from the beginning, came in and saw me crying and demanded to know why. When I told him what had happened he charged out of the room and began to clean house! I had never heard him speak a foul word before and never did after that. I never saw the charge nurse again!

You see, Satan *uses* people. He will camp by your bedside. He laughed at me from the hospital window sill and said, "I didn't get you at the tower, but I will get you before it's over." He never left the room and threatened me all the time. If someone came in he became silent. When I couldn't sleep and had restless nights Satan laughed at me.

As darkness approached, I knew it would be another restless night. Breckenridge was what today we would call a trauma center. The sounds of emergency vehicles filled me with fear that no medication could assuage. Each loud noise took me back to the day of the shooting. Each time I heard an ambulance siren it made me relive the shooting. Each noise brought renewed fears of the still unknown.

Shortly after I began to recover my thoughts turned to home and the huge family of support that had traveled to Austin to visit me. Even my Mother's parents came for a visit. When I think of it now, I believe that was the farthest Grandpa Beeson ever traveled from home! How I loved them and longed to walk the short distance from Mom and Dad's home to their home. Realizing how anxious they all were to support me gave little hope after Satan began his incessant attacks. From there an overwhelming realization that *he* would try any tactic made me realize, in my weakness, I would have to depend on others…especially Mom.

My supporting cast was large. Brenda made daily visits when she could but only for short periods of time. Many friends and extended family would visit me; however there were many times where I could only find a place of hiding under the wings of His Holy Spirit. Dr. Nelson eventually hung a NO VISITORS sign on the door of my room. The early recovery time was long and painful for my family to endure consequently I spent a good bit of time alone. There were few words about the future as it appeared I would have little ability to function as a bread winner much less a man. There were such sick, and wounded people in Breckenridge that sometimes I became desperately involved with their plight. Many families requested prayers for their family members while standing at my door. Every time someone died Satan would remind me that that was going to happen to me! Days and nights were filled with pain and mental oppression. Then a breeze of His Holy Spirit would come into the room. Ahh...the times of refreshment for me and then just as suddenly my nasal cavities were filled with the stench of rotting, infected flesh, the ominous odor of medical treatment and the presence of Satan. My doctor had nurses give me morphine when the pain was unbearable but ceased that later out of fear I would become addicted to it. I understood and fought the pain even with Satan laughing at my suffering.

A good month later, my doctor came to see me. He sat by my bed and said, "Son, we've done all that we can...you will spend your life in a wheelchair. You are alive...be grateful for that." I thought, God has been with me through all of this, he's not going to leave me in this bed. Dad said that I had to think of my ministry. This man who came to help me in a hail of bullets repeated, you have to *live*, and your God is going to help you! Indeed I did! I was hurting physically and emotionally. I prayed, and Jesus comforted me by promising to help me walk. The reality of paralysis set in on the morning I requested my dad to help me in getting out of bed. Jesus had come to me earlier and said, "If you stand up I will help you walk." The next morning while my father was there I said, "Dad, you have to help me stand." Now, no man or woman can stand up after being in bed for over two months...but I was going to do it! Dad came closer to me with tears in his eyes fearing I would fall and feel like a failure. I pleaded with Dad to help me. I reminded Dad of the time he talked to me about a *friend* will never let you down. Slowly he moved me to the edge of the bed and brought my legs around and down until my feet were firmly planted on the floor and could stand. The love of my *father*, this *friend*, took my hand and eased me off the bed. A strange feeling came over me and a warmth sped through my body. I felt God's presence as strength came to my legs. I was shaky and trembling but with his support got my balance and together Dad and I gingerly walked across the floor to the bathroom. Dad cried, and Dr. Nelson, standing in the doorway, put his hands to his face in disbelief. The next time I got up, Dad was in the room and again, he helped me to stand. I needed to use the bathroom. On my own I took small steps to the bathroom with Dad at my right side. I couldn't do anything and asked him to leave me alone in the bathroom...which he did! I could finally do what I went in there to do! Dr. Nelson entered the room and asked, "Where's my patient?" Dad stated, "He's in the bathroom!" Dr. Nelson saw that I was alone, and tears ran down his face!

About 3 am the next morning, *The Cross and the Switchblade* lay by my side. Since I couldn't sleep I wanted to start reading it. When I picked it up a spirit-like being appeared. I saw it but can't describe it...not even to this day.

I asked for a preacher one evening when I couldn't sleep. When he came the first thing I noticed was his shoes. He had nice shoes...funny, the things that stick in your mind. He brought a vial of oil with him and said, "Satan I command you to leave this room in the name of God!" He anointed me with the oil and said, "Jesus, I ask you to let this child sleep." You know you can't buy sleep...but after the preacher left I *did*!

After more surgical procedures and a few more weeks at Breckenridge the surgeon came in with good news and bad news. He told me he thought I could be released to continue the recovery process at home. That was the good news. The bad news was that I would *probably* never be a father. He stated that my colon had been cut in two places from the bullet Whitman hit me with. Other organs had been damaged beyond repair. The thought of going home sounded good but I was scared. Would anyone recognize me? I came into the hospital weighing 185 and was leaving at 118 pounds! I had tubes and bags hanging all over my body...not the way a happy newlywed or want-to-be preacher should look!

Adjusting to this new life at home was hard. Brenda and I

lived with her parents after my release from Breckenridge. We were treated very well as newlyweds but so *much* to adjust to so *quickly*. Brenda was patient with me as she had her own problems to deal with. She is very private and never showed much open affection. However, she never complained about her lingering condition. Her physical injuries soon healed, but she soon realized we had been dealt a hand we had never considered before.

Her strength lay in the fact that she didn't require many things to be content and I thank God for that as there were years of financial and health stress we lived with. Adjusting to this new world was hard. She was fearful of new places, new people, new circumstances. For that matter those same fears affected me in the same way. Brenda's health improved as nature intended with no setbacks, but she struggled with people every week or two. Fear tormented the both of us.

After a few more weeks I drove alone for the first time to a doctor's appointment. I was excited about being able to do this! I didn't need Brenda's parents or anyone to drive me. I felt my independence returning. On the way home from the appointment a car pulled up along side of me. I glanced over to look and saw that the figure's face in the driver's seat was full of rage. Satan again! I can still hear Satan's pleasure when he said, "I've got you *this* time!" He leaned out the window of the car, raising his hand and pointed a gun at me. He fired 2 or 3 times. He didn't hit me or the car. I was so shaken that all I could do was weep and beg God to protect me. Reaching home I was still shaken and fearful. My reaction was to retreat to the bedroom where no one could witness my utter weakness. I prayed to God as He was my hiding place. So many times I needed a hiding place! This was a battle of principalities…not a mere man.

Some two or three months after the shooting, we left Brenda's parents home to live in my home which was about 12 miles southeast of Conroe, TX. I was to continue my recovery there and believe me, it was wonderful. We were blessed with family and friends who arranged a reunion. Everyone gave of themselves in some way. With our focus on healing, Brenda and I had not talked about having children. We had just figured when the time was right we would.

It was almost a year after the shooting incident that I had an appointment with Dr. Nelson. Each time that I was in his office he wanted to see me walk across the room. He was just amazed at the sight. During this visit I asked him about starting a family. I remembered what he had said months earlier but hoped there was a chance he was wrong. He didn't give me much hope. He stated that due to the position of the trajectory and the destructive path it took through my body there probably would be no children. I clung to the word *probably*. In my mind there was still hope. But the prognosis was still hard to swallow for a man wanting to be a father.

Then a new doctor, Dr. Emil Carrol, entered my life and multiple procedures for a benign tumor in my lower abdomen and a corrective procedure to repair holes in my intestines followed. This meant another hospital stay…the longest period since the shooting. I was getting to know the staff very well! The doctors were clever in that they never talked about *my* future. I questioned myself wondering if I even had one! It seemed I had little ability to function as a bread winner let alone a man.

A few months later Brenda and I learned we were expecting a baby. We both were in a state of shock remembering what Dr. Nelson had told me. But then I recalled he used the word *probably!* The pregnancy went well but filled me with anxiety over providing for a family. We had done a little traveling to minister to people, but I would need steady work, and could I fulfill my dream of being a minister? The days and weeks were filled with excitement…especially for Dad. He could hardly wait. When the time came, and Brenda was admitted to the maternity unit, Dr. Carrol gave me medication to knock me out…so much for being the supportive husband!

Our son, Scott, was born April 20, 1968. I received two blessings that day...the birth of our son and the fact that Whitman hadn't taken my chances of being a father away from me.

Months after the birth of Scott and a slow recovery from partial paralysis that still affects me today and numerous surgeries, I began to travel as an evangelist. Traveling with a small baby and another on the way was a very stressful period of time. Churches were very understanding and made many great sacrifices to help and support my family.

It seemed God had smiled partially in my direction. Revival efforts were being blessed and the anointing of God appeared to rest upon our efforts. I remember one meeting in a rural Louisiana setting where we were left to stay in the back of the church building with no bathroom facilities.

Then, God blessed us with Greg on July 23 in '69! You have no idea how these births lifted my confidence to continue my pledge to God. I haven't spoke of this often about how the local Baptist church began to attend revival services and realized the uncomfortable conditions we were in. The minister never knew how those precious people fed and supported us over two weeks. God's people are the best!

With fall approaching in 1969 I was offered and accepted the pastoral position of a small church in Shepherd, Texas. This was only a few miles from my home church where I received my call into the ministry. What an awesome challenge this was in deep East Texas. The attendance in Shepherd remained small for 18 months. But as the revival continued so did the attendance presenting the need to have more room to accommodate the people. As the membership grew, so did the finances that helped us to get up and running! One of the men in the church and I hung sheetrock overhead and I did real damage to surgical procedures done on my insides at the time of the shooting.

My outer stomach would swell until the outside flesh and skin would erupt with vile corruption. In later years,

I had a massive procedure that kept me hospitalized for 28 days. Recovery by now was not as quick as in the past. The blessing came when God blessed this small town of only 1000 with a tremendous congregation and worship facility.

Those days of great revival found us in constant building programs meet the demands of our, once again, growing audience. One remodel and three newly constructed buildings were completed almost entirely by our membership. I take pride in the accomplishments of that period of my ministry. Our greatest accomplishment was a sanctuary that included the choir area and balcony. The people of Shepherd, TX had provided a place for people of all religious persuasions to be saved! Great music, a choir, prayer warriors and new members filled with the Holy Ghost kept the candle burning. I was afforded great opportunities to preach across the United States and South America. As a result of so much travel, we were blessed to know the ministers that could bring even more blessings to our congregation. We heard the best preachers of that era. Many have now gone on to their reward…I pray they rest in peace. Though I have moved on I still have dear friends there.

six

"For I know the plans I have for you", declares the Lord, "plans to prosper you and not to harm you, plans to give you hope and a future."
Jeremiah 29:11

As expected I continued meeting with my doctor to discuss what problems I still wrestled with. With compassion he felt it would help me to return to the scene on the Austin campus. My taste for the campus had soured over time for obvious reasons and also the fact that the campus did *nothing* to assist *any* of the victims...neither those that survived or the families of those who died! My medical bills were astronomical and I'm sure others faced the same thing. Benton Musslewhite, a state Representative talked with me about suing the University but learned the University would fight it feeling no responsibility in the mass shooting.

Thinking the doctor may be right I did return but not until 1978. I stood in the area that I had been shot in and my heart immediately accelerated to 220 beats per minute. In 1976 I had open heart surgery at age 31 so this new heart activity wasn't good. My dad hired a Lear jet ambulance to take me to the Methodist Hospital in Houston. The hospital there had renowned cardio specialists. I stayed two weeks in the hospital before the staff felt secure that my heart rhythm had stabilized, and I could go home. What I thought was astonishing was over 100 ministers were present for the surgery! This and an open-hear surgery in '95 were from the stress I had been under for several years...not the initial shooting at the University. Not as many ministers were present for the surgery in '95 but there were a few that hold my deepest thanks and love. Ed Hall of Mississippi, Lowell Gowins of Illinois, Gary Larson of Florida, and my dear friend Louis Green of Missouri. These are men that have stood by me through thick and thin...the worst and the best of times these past fifty-two years.

As if all that I had been through wasn't enough Satan refused to give up and began attacking my marriage. Just days after my release from the hospital in Houston, I traveled with my dear friend, Louis Green, to visit a mutual friend. Due to the distance we stayed overnight. Upon my return home I was greeted with emptiness. Brenda was gone. Satan had attacked my heart and my home...not my house but *my home*! Louis was with me when I opened the front door to find everything gone! The remaining piece of furniture was the chair my dad had given me during the initial shooting recovery. My mother was sitting in the chair and motioned for me to come to her and began to sing the chorus to *Jesus Loves Me*. She held me close until my sobbing and quaking ceased. Then in the doorway stood my special gifts from God...my sons, Scott and Greg. They seemed so grown up as they stood there. I hold them so dear today. Both of them are better dads than I ever was. I am thankful that God granted that I could raise them in their youthful days.

After 12 years of marriage we divorced, and the court system awarded our sons to my care...they were 8 and 9 years old at the time. Brenda moved back to her parents in Austin. Life without their mother was not easy and let me say I still respect Brenda. We both had issues that haunted us and burdens we had to overcome on our own. God doesn't want the bad things in our lives to dominate the good things that happen in our lives. But if we allow the bad things to have control over us, then God's plan for us will not take place. As Psalm 46:1 says, "God is our refuge and strength. A very present help in trouble."

The ministry, being my ultimate dream position, was very taxing to say the least and sometimes left me feeling empty because of preconceived ideas and notions. Ordination meant so very much to me. After some time of pastoring, I realized my two sons were to me a true gift. I went to the small sanctuary in Shepherd, Texas and lay both of my sons on the church altar. Then I gave them to God. We three are still joined at the altar.

The favor of God opened many doors in the community of Shepherd. Politicians became very aware of our church's ability to elect or to not elect anyone running for office. There were honorable men who asked no special favors; however, they represented us well. Later years found one of my dearest members serving as county commissioner.

When Satan flexes his muscles God provisionally supplies grace to carry on His eternal purpose. One mid-morning the sheriff of our county who also blessed me in many ways, called me from my office with the honking of his horn. Going to the door to see what the cause was the sheriff invited me to take a ride with him to meet a complete stranger. Ramiro Martinez. Ramiro was the police officer that killed Charles Whitman. What a thrill to meet one of my heroes. Ramiro's life took some curves too. He left the Austin Police Department in 1968. In '69 he joined the Texas Department of Public Safety and served as a narcotics agent. In 1973 he became a Texas Ranger working with a task force that discovered the largest marijuana farm ever in San Jacinto County, Texas at the time. His efforts brought about the indictment of George Parr better known as the Duke of Duval County. In 1976 Ramiro sued the producers of the TV film *The Deadly Tower*. The movie painted a negative and racist depiction of his wife. The producers had Mrs. Martinez as a Hispanic woman with issues; when in fact she is a German blue-eyed, blond lady. He won the suit.

Even with all of His blessings there is always an effort of Satan to disrupt the peace and tranquility of spiritual blessing. When it happens it reminds me of Satan's challenge from my window sill in Breckenridge Hospital, room 525, in 1966. After years of mental frustration God sent into my life my beautiful wife Charlene. What joy she brought to my life! She came with two beautiful daughters, two sons-in-law and two little boys. When you add them to our two sons, their wives, three little boys and a little girl… let's see that makes five grandsons and one granddaughter… wow! This makes one sense the grace of God in another period of my swiftly passing life. Get out of my window Satan!

There are days that I still struggle with the pain, but God has been with me through it all and will continue to be beside me. Albert Einstein has stated that there are two ways to live. You can live as if *nothing* is a miracle; or you can live as if *everything* is a miracle. I personally believe that anything in life that is unbelievable or beautiful is part of something bigger than I know. For me it has been God's amazing grace that has seen me through the hell I walked through… I am alive and believe that this has been part of God's plan for me.

God has always given me a heart for pastors and pastoring churches. In 2013, I was asked to pastor a small church in southwest Louisiana. What a precious and loving group we worship with at Calvary Church of Ragley, Louisiana. In the midst of that love Satan again forcefully came against my ministry. Cancer struck Charlene. With her battle of cancer, the last 4 1/2 years, Satan threw his best effort…but he didn't know her tremendous faith nor resolve. During chemotherapy, the loss of her hair and all the days with no answer to the question "why me", she hardly ever missed a church service. She is still our leader in worship and an inspiration to look beyond present circumstances. Her philosophy is that at sunrise things will be better. Days of Bible reading in the solitude of her bedroom gave her the assurance that Jesus would see her through this trial. I shall never forget the evening she began to prepare for our church service, that she called me to the shower. She held in her hand a large portion of her hair. Oh how she sobbed in her heart's brokenness. She insisted I go on to church without her. On the way to church, Satan tried to take control by saying I would find her dead when I returned home! Wrong again, Satan! One of her faithful friends saw her through the removal of the remainder of her hair. I came home to a completely different wife! The hair situation brought to light the describable judgment that rests in some people of faith. No hair, short hair, nor wigs have given her any relief from the antagonistic self-righteous. Many attacks in that region of our lives leaves me saddened by so many who have no continuing understanding nor concern for compassion.

Our Calvary church family have stood by her, and as a consequence, they have strengthened my resolve to continue the battle against my longtime nemesis. Satan has sat in my window sill, ridden in my car, lived in my home and led me into lifelong decisions that haven't spared me nor my family from lasting hurt.

seven

Even to your old age I will be the same, and even to your graying years I will bear you. I have done it and I will carry you and I will deliver you.
Isaiah 46:4

The heart of an old man now quietly and without fanfare searches for the mind of the spirit every day. How grateful I am that there are men and a few spiritual groups, the Apostolic Christian Network, the Apostolic Church of Jesus Christ, and many independent pastors of churches large and small that allow me once again to prove Satan underestimates God's grace. These precious men have received a revelation of restoration.

What I experienced fifty some years ago has left a lasting impression on me. I have a constant reminder of *that* day and the days, months and years afterwards because of the pain I still have after thirteen major surgeries. Not so long ago I was told by my doctors that I needed surgery on my back very close to where the bullet entered…I said no…my age was the determining factor.

God has allowed me to live. He has been a constant, steadfast companion with me. I have a wonderful wife and two sons who love me. I am happy and grateful. My desire is to continue to praise God and serve Him in all the ways that I can. You see…I've done enough dying today. His amazing grace has seen me through these 50 some years and I praise Him for it. No matter what's happened in your life you must believe that Jesus loves you! As the hymn states, "They are weak; but He's so strong. Jesus loves me; the Bible tells me so."

SATAN AT MY WINDOW

epilogue

Adrian Littlefield states, "Of all the victims that I remember, memories of Claire Wilson, no doubt, remains in the foremost of memories. At an interview that was supposed to take place in Austin with CBS 50 years after the shooting I met Claire for the first time since being in the hospital with her. We had gathered to prepare for the memorial service. Claire saw me first and came running to me! She said God had blessed her with a little boy. She had adopted him and felt her life was now complete. It was wonderful to see how happy she was."

In December 2012 Houston McCoy passed away at age 72. In an earlier interview he stated that when he died, he didn't want it written as if he was the hero in the 1966 Austin, TX mass shooting by Charles Whitman. McCoy said there were *many* heroes that day.

Ramiro Martinez, the last of the three men who were on the Observation Deck at the Austin campus of the University of Texas. Officer McCoy and civilian Allen Crum who passed away in 2001, being the other two. In 2006 the city of Austin proclaimed August 1, "Ramiro Martinez Day". This was announced on the 40TH anniversary of the tower shootings. Martinez now resides in New Braunfels, Texas.

Charles A. Whitman, Charles Whitman's father lives a solitary life in a small house in Lantana, South Florida. Suffering from Alzheimer, at 78 still has not come to terms with his son's actions. He often calls it, "an accident." Separated from his third wife he still works as a plumber part time. All three of his sons are deceased. Two died violent deaths and the third from AIDS. He talks of his grandchildren and has a wall full of their pictures. No pictures of his son Charles.

Brenda Littlefield Tice, the first person shot suffered flesh wounds to her left side. She states, "My faith and trust in God has guided me through every situation I have faced. My physical wound healed quickly but my emotional healing took a long time. With the help of God and my family I have been able to put all of that behind me."

Greg Littlefield, son of Adrian and Brenda states, "I never knew the true struggles they went through because they protected us from that day. We were taught to have faith in God and because of that we continue to serve God. My father is one of the strongest men I've ever known. Growing up I've watched him beat all the odds. I wouldn't be the man I am today without his guidance. My father's persistence in life and service to God has only made me want to please God more. I have patterned my life, my marriage to my wife Tammy and father of two sons through Dad's example."

Scott Littlefield, son of Adrian and Brenda states, "Dad's story intrigues me to this day. I can remember as a child coming home after attending a church service that Dad spoke at seeing that he had exerted himself to the point his incisions would reopen and stain his clothing. Many times I have heard people say, never give up. Dad's relentless desire to live and the need to fulfill the calling on his life has kept him from giving up. After seeing God restore Dad time after time, I believe that there is nothing God can't do. Both of our parents taught my brother and me to be respectful, honest and accountable…this has served me well through my personal life and that with my wife and two sons. When I see continued tragedy in our world I still believe in the good of people and know that God can restore and mend lives that have been shaken."

Adrian Littlefield continues to serve God as pastor of Calvary Church in Ragley, LA. He is currently a guest speaker around the world. He lives in Kirbyville, TX with his wife, Charlene and their Border Collie, Bandit.

SATAN AT MY WINDOW

afterward

I was in my mid-teens when the shooting spree in Austin, TX occurred. I was enjoying the summer of 1966 with showing livestock at fairs, being with friends on the weekend and working part time to save for college in a couple of years. I had no knowledge of high-powered fire arms, no knowledge of people who committed terrible crimes, and barely knew the meaning of the war that was going on or the young lives that were serving in our military to preserve the rights and freedoms that this country had.

Then I saw the cover of Time Magazine for that week in 1966 and my whole line of thinking changed about people. Were there really people who could commit such carnage? Does Satan really live and work through people? Yes, he does! It is my thought that Satan is even busier today in our lives considering the horrible acts that are committed by adults and young people who don't even know their victims. Satan hides and often disguises himself. He seems strongest when his existence is denied. If we are honest with ourselves we must admit that in some way, some fashion, we have been introduced to Satan.

My friendship with Adrian Littlefield has been a rewarding experience...one that will not leave my memory or heart. In today's environment of random shootings and mass shootings, *Satan At My Window* will be a help and comfort we all need to survive the deeds of Satan. My wish is that Adrian's story will provide a profound understanding of God's steadfast love in our lives. Through Adrian's experiences *I know* it requires constant prayers and continual faith in God and his personal enrichment to keep demons from influencing our lives and Satan from our windows.

Maureen Hughes works as a private criminal investigator in two states. Her articles have been read in magazines and newspapers. She has served as lay minister in her local church and resides with her family in Illinois and Nevada.

Made in the USA
Columbia, SC
10 March 2019